Joseph (Jay) C. Murphy
1963 Vinton Ave.
Memphis, TN 38104
www.jmurphy.us
Ordering Information:
Quantity sales. Special discounts are available on quantity
purchases by corporations, associations, and others. For details,
contact the publisher at the address above.

Table of Contents

Overview of HTML

Have you ever wanted to create a website? Well it is not as hard as you think it is. All you need to know to create a website is Hypertext Markup Language, also known as "HTML." To get started the first thing you will need to know are tags. HTML tags tell the browser how to read your code. You start HTML tags with "<" and end with ">". Depending on what you want to tell the browser to do, you will put the command in the middle, such as "html." When you want to end the statement, you will put "/" directly before the first "<". So if you were ending a HTML statement it would look like this </html>.

Lets get going on creating your first website. To begin you will need some sort of code editor. A common code editor for Windows computers is Notepad++, and Komodo Edit for Mac. Once you have selected a code editor you will need to create a folder for your files.

So you have created your folder. Now you will want to open your code editor and create a new file. Save the file as whatever you want to call it, but be sure to add ".html" at the end "for example index.html." This is the most common name used for naming you're the homepage of a website. After you complete this you can start on you website. To begin you will want to set up the following:

```
<html>
        <head>
                <title>title</title>
        </head>
                <body>
                        Site content
                </body>
        </html>
```

With all HTML websites you will need to include the <html> tags. This tells your browser that you are using HTML code. All websites have parts of the site that you cannot see, and this is called the <header> tag. The <header> tag will include the title of your website that will show up in the browser, meta tags, and even tracking codes. Meta tags will allow you to insert keywords, descriptions, and other matters. in the header to help search engines index your site. Tracking codes from Google Analytic and other services will allow you to see where your visitors are coming from. In the body <body> tags you will include the objects that go into you website. Anything that is included in the <body> tags will be shown in the browser. Below is an example:

```html
<html>
	<head>
		<title>My Site Title</title>
	</head>

	<body>
		Body of the site goes here
	</body>
</html>
```

Headings

In the body of the website you can use headings to differentiate text from headings. So how do you use headings in your website? Well, there are 6 headings tags you can use: <h1>, <h2>, <h3>, <h4>, <h5>, and <h6>. Each of these headers is a different text size. For demonstration purposes the largest heading is <h1>; the headings gradually get smaller with the smallest being <h6>. The sizes will be similar to this:

h1 - # Heading 1

h2 - ## Heading 2

h3 - ### Heading 3

h4 - #### Heading 4

h5 - ##### Heading 5

h6 - ###### Heading 6

With the heading tags, and any other tags, there are attributes that can change how the heading is displayed on the website. Below are some attributes for headings:

Attribute	Value	Description
align	Righ	This allows you to tell the browser the

	t Left Cent er justi fy	alignment of the text that you want on the website.

Lets go over how to use attributes. Lets say that you have a heading of "<h1>About Me</h1>", and you want it on the right side of the page. You will type out the heading tag as you normally do, but you will just add a space, then put align="". In the quotation marks you will put the value you want. So the heading will look similar to this: "<h1 align="right">About Me </h1>".

Body

The body of your html document is what you will see on your website.

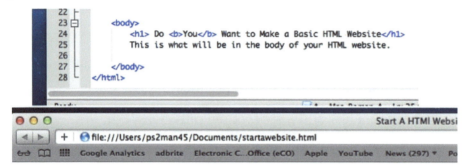

In the body you can include any thing that you need to be shown on your website. With the <body> tag there are some attributes that will let you customize the body of the website. Below are some common attributes that are used in web design.

Attribute	Value	Description
background	link	Tell the browser what background image you want
bgcolor	Hex code Color name	Tells the browser what is the image color you want displayed
text	Hex code Color name	Tells the browser the font color

6

alink	Hex code Color name	Tellls the browser the color of active links
link	Hex code Color name	Tells the browser the color of unvisited links
vlink	Hex code Color name	Tells the browser the color of visited link

As with any attribute you will put it in the opening <body> tag, and then put the attribute after body with a space like this <body attribute="value">. With the attribute background you will put the link to the file you want as the background in quotations, <body background="background.png">, you have to make sure that you include the type of file it is in the example above.

As you can see some of the attributes you will have to include the color name of the hex code. A hex code is a code that is used in HTML to tell the browser what code you want to use. Some examples of hex codes are:

Red	#ff0000
Orange	#ffA500
Yellow	#ffff00
Olive	#808000
Green	#008000

If you want more hex code you can do a basic search on any search engine for *"HTML color codes."* When using hex code you will want to use them in the following way <body text="#ff0000">. You can also name the color <body text="red">. Now that you know what goes into the body of your HTML file you can start on your website and customize it in a simple way.

Links

       One of the most important parts of websites are links, and most people will want to put their favorite links on their website. To put a website link on your website you will need to use the <a> tag. With the <a> tag you will need to know the *"href"* attribute. This attribute will allow you to put the URL to the desired webpage. As with any other attribute, you will need to format it. This attribute will look like this: <a href=http://www.jmurphynation.com>, but you will need to put the title in between the opening and ending <a> tags.

       When you are finished with your link it should look like this with the webpage you are linking to: <a href=http://www.jmurphynation.com>Jmurphy Nation</a>. If you want the link to show up in a new window or tab, you can use an attribute to do this too. Here are some attributes that you can use to customize link tags.

Attributes	Value	Description
href	URL	Tells the browser the URL that the link goes to
target	_blank _self	Tells the browser where to open the link

So you are probably wondering what do the values that go with the Attribute target mean. Well lets start off with the two most common values, _blank and _self. The _blank value will allow you to have the linked website or document open in another window or tab. The _self value will allow you to open the website or document that you linked to in the same window or tab.

Images

Time to learn how to put images in your website. First of all, you will need to know the tag you need. In placing an image on your website you will use the <img> tag. With the image tag you will use the following attributes to customize your image.

Attribute	Value	Description
src	URL	Tells the browser where the image is located
alt	text	Tells the browser a description of your image
align	top bottom middle left right	Tells the browser where to place the image on the website
height	Number of pixels	Tells the browser the height of the image you want
width	Number of pixels	Tells the browser the width of the image you want

Lets show you how to use those attributes now. For demonstration purposes I am going to use the *"src"* and the *"align"* attributes. You will first start off with the <img> tag, and find the link of the image you want to use. With the *"src"* attribute you can use an image already on the web with its link, or you can use a image file in your HTML folder. Just make sure that you put the file type at the end like image.png. When using an image from the web you will just need to copy the address into the quotation

11

marks. So it should look like this if you are using a image in the HTML folder: <img src="image.pnh" />, and if you are using a linked image from the web it will look like this:

<img src="http://jmurphynation.com/wpcontent/uploads/image.jpg" />.

When adding another attribute to the <img> tag all you need to do is put a space after your last attribute: <img src="image.png" align="left" />. As you probably have noticed, there is no ending tag for this, unlike the hyperlink tags and other ones. There is no need for one, all you have to do is place a space at the last attribute and end it with />. With the other attributes they will follow the same pattern: attribute="value".

Paragraphs and Formatting

Now lets learn how to place paragraphs into your website. The first thing that you will need to know is the paragraph tag. The tag you will be using for this will be <p>. Once you get done with your first paragraph, you will need to go to the next line; you can accomplish this by using the line break tag <br>. This tag will act like the enter button if you want to have space between you paragraphs. For example-

    <p>

        This is the first line

        This is the second line

        This is still the second line

        This is the third line

    </p>

Lets get started with some formatting now. With an assortment of HTML tags you can do many of the things you can do with a word processor. When working with the font of your paragraph you will use the <font> tag. The way you will use the <font> tag is:

`<p>`

`<font>`

This is what will be in your paragraph.

`</font>`

`</p>`

Some of the attributes that you will use are:

Attribute	Value	Description
size	Font size	Tells the browser what will the font size of the text
face	Font of choice	Tells the browser what font to use
color	color	Tells the browser of the color of the text

As with any attribute you will place it in the opening tag with a space after the tag name. so it will look similar to this: <font size="5" face="fontname">. With HTML you can also customize the text making it bold and italicized for example.

Tag	Description
`<b>`	**Bolds the text**
`<i>`	*Italicized the text*
`<u>`	<u>Underline the text</u>
`<big>`	Makes the text bigger
`<strong>`	Makes the text stronger
`<small>`	Makes the text smaller
`<em>`	Emphasizes the text
`<sub>`	This tag will $_{subscript}$ the text
`<sup>`	This tag will ^{superscript} the text
`<li>`	• This will make a list • ….

About the Author

Jay Murphy is a freshman in college at the University of Memphis, and is majoring in computer science. He writes a tech blog on the newest technology, and is particularly interested in reviewing the newest Apple products. In his spare time Jay enjoys playing paintball, and playing the newest video games.

I appreciate each and every one of you for taking time out of

your day to read this. If you have an extra moment, I would like to hear what you think about this. You can post a comment on http://www.jmurphynation.com/ebook, or contact me by an email.

Joseph (Jay) Murphy III

jmurphy@jmurphynation.com

Exercises

1.If you have a file named website what extension would at the end of it?

2.Write out the format of an HTML document.

3.What do you include in the Header, and body section of the HTML document?

<u>Header</u>

<u>Body</u>

4.Write the size of the headings from smallest to greatest.

5.With an <h1> tag assign it to be centered.

6.With the HTML structure you answered to in the previous question display your name on the screen with the <h1> tag.

7.Will everything you place in the body tag be displayed on the screen?

8.Write down HTML code that will have a background of black and text color of white. Use the <h1> tag in the previous question for your text.

9.List three of your favorite colors, and then find the hex codes for the.

10.Using your favorite website or jmurphynation.com make a link to the website that you have picked.

11.You have an image named header.png. Using the img tag write down the complete image tag and center.

12. What HTML tag do you use to go to a new line?

13. Write a sentence in a paragraph tag and format it with you choosing.

Answers

1. ".*html*"

2. ```html
   <html>
           <header>
           </header>
           <body>
           </body>
   </html>
   ```

3. Head- information tags, tracking tags and etc. Example: `<meta>` and `<script>`

   Body – anything that you would want displayed in the browser Example: `<p>`, `<b>`, and `<img>` tags

4. `<h6>,<h5>…<h2>,<h1>`

5. `<h1 align="center" >`

6. `<h1 align="center" >Your Name</h1>`

7. Yes

8. ```html
   <html>
           <header>
           </header>
           <body background="black" color="white">
                   <h1 align="center" >Your Name</h1>
           </body>
   </html>
   ```

9. Hex code can be found on computerhope.com/htmcolor.htm

10. <a
    href="http://www.jmurphynation.com">JmurphyNation</a
    >
11. <img src="header.png" />
12.
13. Place the sentence you
    wrote here

www.ingramcontent.com/pod-product-compliance
Lightning Source LLC
Chambersburg PA
CBHW041151050326
40689CB00004B/724